Guy Fawkes

by
David Fermer

Ernst Klett Sprachen
Stuttgart

Augmented:
Zu dieser Geschichte gibt es auch das Hörbuch und einen Wortschatztrainer
für alle Vokabeln im Glossar. Um das Hörbuch bzw. den Wortschatztrainer
herunterzuladen, musst du zuerst die Klett-Augmented-App installieren.
Halte dann die Kamera deines Smartphones oder Tablets jeweils über
die erste Seite jeder Episode, um diese zu scannen. Wenn du auch die
Vokabeln zu den *Character-Seiten* und den *Additional information* üben
möchtest, scanne zusätzlich noch die Seiten 4 und 30.

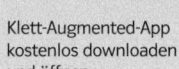

Klett-Augmented-App
kostenlos downloaden
und öffnen

Bilderkennung starten
und die entsprechenden
Seiten scannen

Inhalte laden, direkt
nutzen oder speichern

1. Auflage   1 ⁷ ⁶ ⁵ ⁴ | 2021 20 19 18

Alle Drucke dieser Auflage sind unverändert und können im Unterricht nebeneinander
verwendet werden.
Die letzte Zahl bezeichnet das Jahr des Druckes. Das Werk und seine Teile sind urheberrech-
tlich geschützt. Jede Nutzung in anderen als den gesetzlich zugelassenen Fällen bedarf der
vorherigen schriftlichen Einwilligung des Verlags.

Autor: David Fermer
Redaktion: Don Haupt
Layoutkonzeption: Elmar Feuerbach
Umschlaggestaltung: Sandra Vrabec
Grafik: Matthias Pflügner, Berlin
Druck und Bindung: Medienhaus Plump GmbH, Rheinbreitbach
Printed in Germany

ISBN 978-3-12-572266-8

Contents

Thanks to the annual celebration of Bonfire Night on November 5th, most people in Britain know the name Guy Fawkes – a historical figure immortalised by the symbolic burning of an effigy of him in villages and towns all over Britain. The story behind this somewhat brutal tradition is both complex and exciting. It is known simply as The Gunpowder Plot. Here is a short introduction to the key people involved in the plan to blow up Parliament and kill the King of England:

Guy Fawkes

Robert Catesby

Guy Fawkes was a soldier who began his career fighting for the Spanish army against the Dutch in the Eighty Years' War. During this time, he became an expert in explosives and later used this knowledge in the plot to blow up the House of Lords.

Robert Catesby was the leader of the Gunpowder Plot and mastermind behind the conspiracy. Catesby spent many years bringing together the most powerful Catholics in the country in the hope of replacing the Protestant king with a Catholic-friendly heir.

Francis Tresham

Lord Monteagle

Francis Tresham was one of the thirteen plotters involved in the Gunpowder Plot. He is often given the blame for exposing the Gunpowder Plot, though many historians say there is no real proof of this.

Lord Monteagle, whose real name was William Parker, was a Catholic English peer who exposed the Gunpowder Plot after he received an anonymous letter from one of the plotters warning him of the attack.

King James

Robert Cecil

King James I was born in 1566, the son of Mary, Queen of Scots. When he was eight months old, his father was murdered and his mother was put into prison. He never saw her again. She was later executed by her cousin, Elizabeth I of England. Although James' mother was Catholic, James was never close to her and grew up a Protestant. At the age of one he became King of Scotland. Later, in 1603, he became King of England and Ireland as well.

Robert Cecil was one of the most powerful politicians in England at the time of James I. His father, William Cecil, had been the chief advisor to Queen Elizabeth I. Robert became Secretary of State under Elizabeth and remained in power under James I. He was also known as the "spymaster".

The Undercroft

The House of Lords was the English Parliament. Its members were Lords rather than democratically elected politicians. In 1605 Westminster was quite different than it is today. It was surrounded by a wall, a bit like a small city in itself. Within these walls there were shops and inns and – most famously – a huge cellar known as an "undercroft" where shopkeepers could store their goods. The conspirators of the Gunpowder Plot used this undercroft to store their gunpowder until the State Opening of Parliament.

" Hey, check this out!" Liam pointed at a scarecrow, whose head was sticking out of a pile of rubbish.

"Cool!" said Jenson.

The boys pulled the scarecrow out of the pile. Apart from a missing arm, he was in pretty good shape.

"I can ask my dad for some clothes," said Liam, wiping some dirt off the scarecrow's face. "He's about the same size."

The two boys often came to the local rubbish dump looking for unusual items. It was amazing what they found: old TVs which still worked, radios, coats, and wellington boots. They took their findings home and cleaned them up. The scarecrow was perfect for tonight's bonfire.

Back home, the boys cleaned up the scarecrow and repaired his arm. They dressed him in a shirt and trousers and gave him gloves and shoes and a hat for his head. Then they went into town to buy him a mask. The mask they bought had narrow, black eyes and an evil smile.

That afternoon the boys carried their new doll down to the village green, where wood and branches were piled up high to make a bonfire, waiting to be lit. Liam threw the doll over his shoulder and carried it to the top of the pile. As night fell, people began to gather on the green. Someone lit the paper at the base of the bonfire, and soon the wood was blazing wildly. The boys watched the flames rise towards the masked figure above. They heard people talk around them.

"Doesn't he look scary!" they said. "I've seen his mask on TV."

As the scarecrow's legs caught fire, a little girl began to cry. "That man is going to die!" she wept.

Her father put his arm around her. "Don't worry," he said. "*He*'s just a Guy. He tried to kill the King of England a long time ago. His name was Guy Fawkes. This is his punishment."

It didn't matter what her father said, the girl carried on crying. No one in the world deserved to die like this.

" Hear the words of the Lord and your soul will be saved!"

The young boy loved listening to the preachers in the streets of York. Their words painted pictures in his head: heaven and hell, fire and salvation, death and glory. The Bible had the best stories ever.

"Come on, Guy, let's go," said the boy's father. Actually Denis Bainbridge wasn't his real father. Guy's father had died when he was eight, but his mother had remarried.

As Guy and Denis walked home through the streets of York, Guy watched the people around him: farmers bringing their goods to the city, men singing drunken songs outside the taverns, women busy with their daily chores. On Stonegate Street, he saw a group of soldiers break down the door of a house. They charged into the building and dragged out a man.

"What are they doing?" Guy asked, shocked by what he was seeing.

The soldiers began to beat the man on the street, shouting at him.

"It's none of our business," said Denis, as he pulled Guy away.

Later, in the safety of their own home, Denis took the boy to one side and explained what had happened. "Did you see the cross around his neck? The cap on his head? That man was a Catholic priest."

"But why did they beat him?" asked Guy.

"Because Catholics are hated in this country."

Denis was a Catholic. Guy's mother, too. Guy had become a Catholic after his father's death. His teachers at school were also Catholic, though they told the children not to talk about their religion beyond the school gates. More and more people were joining the Church of England, and Catholics were hated all over the country.

"Never tell anyone you're Catholic," Denis warned the boy. "Otherwise you might end up like the priest we saw today."

The next day, on his way to school, Guy saw the priest again. He was sitting on a platform, his hands and feet locked into wooden stocks. "They will kill him later," said Denis before moving on. Guy closed his eyes and muttered a prayer. He didn't want to die like that.

Under the cover of dark, four soldiers crept up to the city gates, carrying small barrels of gunpowder. The soldiers guarding the city walls heard a sound below and called out, "Who's there?"

The men froze down below, hoping the night-time fog would hide them. If the guards sounded the alarm, they were dead. Their leader whistled into his hands like an owl.

"It was nothing," said the soldiers on the city wall.

The group leader showed his men where to put the barrels. Once in place, he connected them with a fuse before signalling to retreat.

As quiet as mice, the men backed away from the city walls. Their leader carefully laid the fuse over the ground. Soon they were back at camp. The captain was waiting for them.

"Is everything ready?" he asked in Spanish. The group leader nodded. "Well done, Fawkes! If this works, we can take Calais."

At dawn the next day, Fawkes lit the fuse and watched it burn until the four barrels detonated in a gigantic explosion. The Spanish soldiers took out their weapons and ran towards the city of Calais.

"Your excellency, Señor Fawkes is here!"

After the fall of Calais, Guy Fawkes was called to the Spanish commander, Don Luis de Velasco, who was living in the old town hall.

"Good work, Fawkes!" Don Luis praised him. "King Philip will be very happy with you."

"I am not fighting for King Philip," said Guy Fawkes. "I am fighting for the Pope." Don Luis smiled. "The Spanish crown and the Pope often have similar interests."

"I have no interest in Spain," said Fawkes. "I am an Englishman. I want to return my country to the hands of the Catholic Church."

"Whatever your reasons," said Don Luis. "I want to make you a captain." Guy Fawkes was surprised. An English captain in the Spanish army?

"This is not the last of our battles, my friend. As long as you fight for our army, you must have a title and a Spanish name. From now on, we will call you Guido. Guido Fawkes."

Guy Fawkes walked through the empty streets of London, his hand resting on the hilt of his sword. London was a dangerous place at this time of night. It was dark. There were robbers everywhere.

He soon found the place he was looking for: an inn called the *Duck and Drake*. Inside men were drinking by the fire. Women danced between the tables. When the innkeeper saw Fawkes, he approached him and said, "Follow me."

The innkeeper led Guy to a room at the back of the inn where four men were waiting for him. The youngest, Robert Catesby, jumped to his feet and embraced the newcomer. "Guido! Welcome back to England," he said and introduced the other men. "Thomas Wintour, John Wright and Thomas Percy." "Why did you ask me to come here tonight?" asked Fawkes.

Robert Catesby closed the door. "We have a plan," he said, lowering his voice. "We want this country to be Catholic again. We will kill the King of England at the State Opening of Parliament."

"The king has not kept his promise," Percy continued. "Life is even more difficult for Catholics than before."

"What is your plan?"

"Percy will rent a house near Parliament," Catesby explained. "Spanish friends can supply us with gunpowder which we will transport from my house to Percy's house. There we can place it under the House of Lords ..."

"And you want me to light the fuse?" Fawkes interrupted.

"We cannot do this without you, Guido."

"How can we place the gunpowder under Parliament?"

"You will live with Percy, posing as his servant. We will dig a tunnel from his house into the cellars," Catesby explained. "But before we discuss the details, you must decide: Will you join us?"

Fawkes did not have to think for long. "I will," he said.

"Then let us swear an oath of secrecy." Catesby took out a Catholic prayer book and placed it on the table. "None of us shall ever say a word of this to anyone outside this room, so help us God!"

Catesby's plan worked. Fawkes moved into Percy's house in the role of Percy's servant. Every week, under the cover of darkness, Fawkes took a small boat and crossed the River Thames to Catesby's house in Lambeth. There, Catesby's servants helped him load up his boat with barrels of gunpowder.

"How many do you have now?" Catesby asked, after Fawkes and his friends had spent several weeks transporting barrels across the river.

"Twenty," said Fawkes. "I need ten more. Fifteen would be better."

"Then you will get sixteen, my friend! We must be ready soon. Parliament will be opening in June. Will you be able to make it by then?"

"We are making good progress with the tunnel," Fawkes informed him. "By God's will, we will be ready for the State Opening."

Returning to the north bank, Thomas Wintour and John Wright helped Fawkes carry the barrels back to Percy's house. They had only just brought the barrels into the house when there was a knock at the door. The men froze as they heard a voice. "Percy, are you there?"

Fawkes and his friends quickly hid the barrels in the cellar before Fawkes answered the door. Standing on the doorstep was Percy's patron, the Earl of Northumberland. Two of the king's bodyguards were with him.

"Who are you?" Northumberland asked suspiciously.

"My name is John Johnson, my lord. I am Master Percy's housekeeper."

The earl seemed satisfied with Fawkes' explanation. "I am looking for Percy. Is he at home?"

"I'm afraid not," Guy Fawkes said. "He's in the Palace of Westminster." This was truer than the Earl of Northumberland could have guessed.

"Tell him I was looking for him," said Northumberland and turned to go. "I have a job for him," he added before leaving.

Percy came home from the palace with good news. "I have rented a storage room in the cellars under the House of Lords. We do not need the tunnel. Tomorrow we can start putting the barrels into their final position!"

"Close the door, Guido!" said Catesby as Fawkes entered the room. Twelve men sat huddled around the table in the back room of the *Duck and Drake*.

"Who are these men?" asked Fawkes, surprised.

"Some of the most powerful Catholics in the country," Catesby explained.

"King James has postponed the State Opening until November," Percy continued. "After we kill him, James' Protestant friends will try to take the throne for themselves. Gunpowder alone is not enough. These men will help us build an army."

Fawkes looked into the faces of his fellow conspirators. He recognised Robert Keyes and Ambrose Rookwood and Francis Tresham. Francis looked pale. Fawkes could see fear in his eyes, but he couldn't tell whether it was fear of the dangerous mission ahead or fear of the changes that would come about as a result. He knew these were good men, but did they really have the courage to do this?

Keyes stood up to speak. "Many Catholic friends will be at the State Opening," he said. "Lords Vaux, Montague and Stourton. Tresham's brother-in-law, Lord Monteagle, too. We should warn them."

"Nobody will be warned!" said Catesby angrily. "We have sworn an oath of secrecy. We risk losing everything."

"But will God forgive us for killing innocent men?" Keyes asked.

"We cannot choose who the gunpowder will kill," said Catesby. "These men have chosen to work for King James. If they die, they will die for a good cause. God is on our side."

"My brother-in-law hates King James as much as we do," said Tresham. "He would never betray us."

"We could wound him instead," Roockwood suggested. "We could attack him and stop him from attending the State Opening."

"No!" Catesby grabbed Tresham by the collar of his coat and shook him, his face red with anger. "No one will warn Lord Monteagle. No one will speak of our plan outside of this room. He who does, dies!"

Lord Monteagle stood at the window of his house in Hoxton and watched the birds fly overhead. It was the end of his summer break, and soon he would be heading back to London.

He saw a horseman come galloping through the gates and ride up to the house. He heard his servants open the door, but before they came to announce the visitor, he saw the horseman return to his horse and ride away. There was a knock at his door. His servant came in holding a small, sealed envelope. "A letter for you, my lord. From a friend, the messenger said."

Lord Monteagle took the envelope, broke the wax seal with a knife and handed the letter back to his servant. "Read it," he said.

> "My Lord, out of the love I bear to you, I would advise you to devise some excuse not to attend this parliament. Those present will receive a terrible blow, but they shall not see who hurts them. The danger is passed as soon as you have burned this letter..."

"Elizabeth! Elizabeth! Where are you?"

Lord Monteagle's wife was getting dressed for dinner when her husband burst into her chamber, waving the letter in the air. He hadn't burned it as its writer had wished. "There is a plot to kill the king!"

Elizabeth smiled. "What a wonderful idea!"

"This is not a joking matter, my dear. I believe there is a plan to blow up Parliament!"

Elizabeth continued to smile. "Then I suggest you are ill that day."

"What if the plan goes wrong? What if the king finds out that I knew all along?" said Monteagle. "You don't understand. This is an opportunity."

Monteagle's wife looked at her husband quizzically. "How?"

"If I warn the king, I can win influence in his court," Monteagle explained. "He will reward me. With the king listening to me, I can really help Catholics in this country. Killing the king won't help at all."

Elizabeth's eyes sparkled with delight. "Then do it! Do it today!"

Robert Cecil was an old hand at the game of politics. His father had been a close advisor to Queen Elizabeth I, and he had organised the smooth succession of Elizabeth's nephew, James, to the throne. As Secretary of State, he knew everything that was going on.

When he heard that Lord Monteagle wanted to speak to him, he knew it was a serious matter. Monteagle was shown into Cecil's chambers at Whitehall, where he gave Cecil the anonymous letter. Cecil read it in silence.

"Do you recognise the handwriting?" he asked after finishing.

"I do not."

"Is it from the hand of your wife's brother?"

Again Monteagle shook his head. It was a terrifying thought that Francis might be involved in the plot.

"I swear to God it is not, my lord. All I can do is give you this letter. I cannot give you the man who wrote it. I hope His Majesty will remember me for this."

"I'm sure he will," said Cecil with a smile. "I'm sure he will."

Cecil didn't show the letter to James at first. James was away on a hunting trip. Instead he tried to find out who was behind the plot by using his network of spies. He knew that Thomas Wintour had been in Spain trying to win support from the Spanish crown, but to arrest him now would look bad without evidence. Besides, there were others working with him. Cecil wanted to catch them all.

But Cecil's spies were not able to help him. By the time the king returned from his hunting trip, Cecil still hadn't found out who wrote the letter. He decided to ask King James to cancel the State Opening.

"We must make a full search of the House of Lords," said King James after reading the letter. "When we catch these traitors, I want full confessions! I want them to renounce the Catholic faith and swear loyalty to me before we ..." The king stopped in mid-sentence.

"Before we do what, Your Majesty?" Cecil asked.

"Before we have them killed," said the king.

Fawkes carried the last barrel of Spanish gunpowder into the cellar under the House of Lords. He placed it next to the thirty-five other barrels and hid them behind a pile of wood.

He heard voices echo through the cellar. There had been a lot of activity over the past two nights. Fawkes had been stopped by soldiers the evening before. He had explained that he was Thomas Percy's servant and the soldiers had let him go, but now there were more of them. Did the king know about the plot?

Fawkes had just put the last log into place when someone spoke to him from behind. "You there! What are you doing?"

Fawkes turned and raised his hat. "John Johnson. Servant to Thomas Percy. I was just collecting some firewood for the fire at home."

The soldiers looked at the wood. They looked at him from head to foot. "A fine hat for a servant," said the captain. "And a sword, too. Why do you carry a sword, Mr Johnson? What are you scared of down here?"

"The streets of London are dangerous at night," said Fawkes.

"Search him!" ordered the captain.

The guards stepped into the cellar. Fawkes put his hand on his sword, ready to attack.

"Give me your weapon!" said the captain, holding out his hand. Fawkes hesitated. He had no chance of beating four soldiers. He drew his sword and handed it to the captain.

Two of the soldiers searched through Fawkes' pockets while the fourth began looking around the cellar. It didn't take him long to find something.

"Look, captain!" He pushed a pile of coal aside and revealed a barrel of gunpowder. He knocked over the stack of logs. Behind them were even more barrels.

"Look at this!" One of the men pulled a piece of cord out of Fawkes' pocket. The other found a small box. "A fuse! And matches!"

The captain drew his sword and held it to Fawkes' chest. "You, Mr Johnson, are under arrest!"

" Tell us who you are working with!"

"My name is John Johnson. I am the servant of Thomas Percy."

"You are lying! Tell us your real name!"

"My name is John Johnson. I am the servant of Thomas Percy," repeated Guy Fawkes. His nose was bleeding. His hair was wet with sweat. His bones and stomach hurt. He was hungry and thirsty.

"We know you are a soldier!" said the Lord Chief Justice. "You have scars on your chest and arms. Tell us your real name! Are you working for the Spanish crown?"

Fawkes raised his head and looked out of the narrow window to the River Thames outside the Tower of London. The sky was dark with clouds. A black raven landed on the windowsill and looked into the room. Fawkes repeated his statement for the hundredth time: "My name is John Johnson. I am the servant of Thomas Percy."

"You are a fool!" said the Lord Chief Justice and left the room angrily. "My horse!" he ordered outside. "I have to speak to King James!"

"Yes, my lord, he is still saying his name is John Johnson," explained the Chief Justice as he informed the king about his progress. "But he has admitted to his plan to kill you."

Robert Cecil listened carefully to the Chief Justice's report. The prisoner in the Tower of London could only be a soldier. How else could he have known how to handle so much gunpowder? Thirty-six barrels would have blown up the entire building!

Cecil knew what the king had to do.

"If he is not talking, then you will have to persuade him," said James.

The Chief Justice looked at the king in surprise. "You mean, torture?"

"Start with a little gentle persuasion," suggested the king. "Use what methods are necessary."

"But, my lord, torture is forbidden …" the Chief Justice began.

"… except by the king's order," Cecil interrupted. "Put John Johnson on the rack until he talks. We want names. All of them!"

The Lord Chief Justice bowed. "Very well, sire."

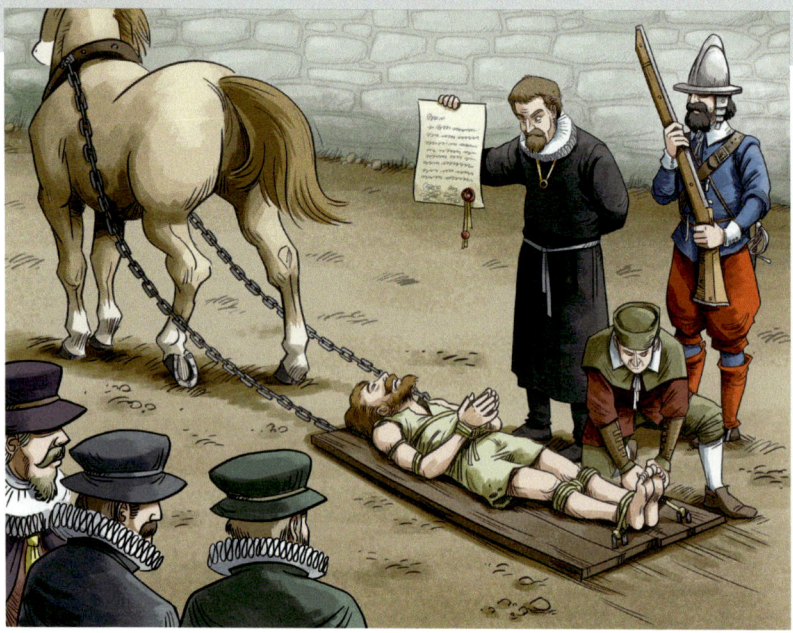

Guido Fawkes signed his name at the bottom of the confession. His hand was shaking so badly that he could hardly hold the quill.

"Take him to Westminster!" ordered the Lord Chief Justice.

Fawkes didn't care what happened to him now. He had suffered so much pain on the rack and spent so many hours hanging from the wall that he felt like he was dead already.

The soldiers carried him downstairs, where they took him into the yard and tied him to a wooden panel attached to a horse. The horseman whipped the horse and Fawkes was dragged out of the Tower.

Outside, crowds of people stood in the streets, watching the spectacle. The pain was too much for Fawkes to bear. He closed his eyes and fell unconscious. The next thing he knew, someone was pouring a bucket of cold water over his head and pulling him to his feet.

"This is the man who plotted to blow up the King of England," announced a man in a loud voice. "A traitor!"

Fawkes opened his eyes. He was standing in front of a wooden stage. A large crowd was gathered around him. He could see Parliament to one side. The very place he had planned to blow up.

"Tell them this is true!" ordered his executioner. "Tell them what a traitor you are!"

Fawkes took a deep breath and shouted into the crowd, "My name is Guido Fawkes. I planned to kill the Scottish King! It is a shame I did not succeed!"

The crowd booed. "It's time to meet your maker," said the executioner and pointed to the gallows on the stage. The executioner pushed Fawkes towards the gallows. He took one step, then another, and another. He was so weak he could hardly walk. He felt the heavy weight of the noose settle around his neck.

Hanging almost to the point of death was only the first part of this gruesome execution. Guy simply could not face any more pain. In a final effort, desperate, he jumped. The crowd gasped. He felt his neck snap and break. Then there was nothing.

Balls of fire exploded over Canterbury Cathedral, lighting up the night sky. The Archbishop, leader of the Church of England, sat in front of his beloved cathedral. Next to him, Robert Cecil was drinking a glass of wine. Around them, the crowd was dancing to music. The Archbishop's servants were handing out food at several stalls around the square. Beer and wine flowed like water.

"A wonderful idea, this celebration!" said the Archbishop. "A day of thanksgiving one year after the attempted assassination of the king."

"A day to remember God's intervention," agreed Robert Cecil, watching the festivities. "The bonfires are a symbol of the dangers which King James survived."

"Magnificent!" said the Archbishop. "Something the people of England will never forget."

Children danced and sang nursery rhymes. *"Remember, remember, the fifth of November! Gunpowder, treason and plot!"*

Two boys approached the Archbishop carrying the dummy of a man. The Archbishop's soldiers stopped them.

"We have a question, my lord!" called one of the boys. The Archbishop waved to his soldiers. The boys came closer.

"What do we have here?" asked the Archbishop.

"This is Guy Fawkes," said one of the boys. "Can we put him on the bonfire?"

"You want to burn him?" asked the Archbishop, shocked.

The second boy waved his fist angrily. "He tried to kill the King of England. He deserves to die!"

The Archbishop exchanged a look with Cecil. "Very well!" he said.

The boys took their dummy and put it on the bonfire. The crowd gathered around. As the flames reached the dummy, people began to cheer and sing.

"Guy, guy, guy! Poke him in the eye! Put him on the bonfire, and there let him die!"

Before long, the Guy was burnt to ashes and nothing remained except for the smoke in the sky.

THE END

Historical background

The Gunpowder Plot took place more than four hundred years ago, at a time when the world was a very different place than it is today. It is therefore rather alarming to see certain parallels between the events of 1605 and the world today. Effectively, the Gunpowder Plot was a terrorist act motivated by religious belief and a deep sense of oppression. Seen from today's perspective, Guy Fawkes could be considered a fundamentalist terrorist. Of course he saw himself in a very different light: as a freedom fighter fighting for the true God and the greater good.

The religious situation in England in the 16th and early 17th century was extremely complex. In 1534, King Henry VIII, a devout Catholic, separated the English Church from Rome and was excommunicated by the Pope. This followed a long story in which Henry had first requested permission from the Pope to marry his brother's widow, only then to request permission to divorce her. She had failed to give him a male heir to the throne and Henry desperately wanted a son. This was too much for the Pope. To solve his problem, Henry left the Catholic Church and founded his own church, known as The Church of England. This change created a massive religious divide in the state of England. Many people wanted to remain Catholic. To achieve success in establishing his new Church, Henry introduced laws that weakened the power of Catholics in England and called for allegiance to the king as head of the Church of England. After Henry died – and following the short reigns of his son, Edward, and daughter, Mary – Henry's second daughter, Elizabeth, became Queen of England. Elizabeth introduced a period of stability into the divided country and strengthened Protestant power. When Queen Elizabeth died in 1603, James became king. Because James was the son of a Catholic woman, Mary, Queen of Scots, many Catholics in England hoped the situation would become better for them. But James was Protestant and a weak king. The country was not run by him, but by court advisors – in particular Robert Cecil, his chief advisor, who hated Catholics. Instead of making the situation better for Catholics in England, James made them even worse, making Catholicism almost illegal. Angry and disappointed, some of the more influential Catholics of the country got together to plan James' murder and replace him with James' nine year old daughter. This was the beginning of the Gunpowder Plot.

The life of Guy Fawkes

Guy Fawkes was born in 1570, one of four children, to Edward Fawkes and his wife, Edith, in York. His parents and grandparents were active members of the Church of England, but when Guy was eight years old, his father died and things began to change. Guy's grandparents on his mother's side were Catholic. His mother met and married Denis Bainbridge, also a Catholic, and she soon began to revert to the Catholic faith. In Fawkes' school, several teachers were Catholic, all of whom practised their religion in secret.

After finishing school and spending a few years working for the Montague family in Sussex, Fawkes packed his bags at the age of twenty-one and travelled to continental Europe where he joined the Spanish army and spent the next ten years fighting against the Dutch. At the time, countries like Holland and Belgium, known as the Low Countries, belonged to the Spanish Crown. Protestantism was popular in the Low Countries, and their fight to gain independence from Spain was both a religious and political one. After proving his skills with gunpowder and being made captain in the Spanish army, Fawkes travelled to Spain to find support for a Catholic rebellion in England. It was during this time that he adopted the Italian name "Guido" which he used several years later when signing his confession after the failure of the Gunpowder Plot.

Unable to find support in Spain, Fawkes came back to England and got involved in the Gunpowder Plot through its leader, Robert Catesby. It was almost 18 months from the first meeting with Catesby to his arrest at midnight on November 5th. After his capture, Fawkes was in prison for two months. He was tortured until he signed his confession and was then put on trial together with seven other plotters. The outcome was never in doubt. Found guilty of high treason, Fawkes faced a terrible death: he was sentenced to be hanged, drawn, and quartered. That means that the prisoner was hanged by the neck almost to the point of death, then, while still alive, his genitals were cut off and burned in front of him and the stomach was cut open to remove the inner organs. Finally he was beheaded and the body chopped into four pieces. (Women were burned at the stake instead.) Fawkes was the last member of the Gunpowder Plot to be hanged and quartered and was spared much pain by what may have been an accident or an attempt to kill himself. While climbing the ladder to the gallows, Fawkes jumped or fell and broke his neck. His lifeless body was still quartered after his death. Guy Fawkes lived and died in brutal times.

Exercises

Episode 1

Choose the correct answer.

1. Liam asked his dad for…
   a) ☐ some clothes.
   b) ☐ a mask.
   c) ☐ some money.

2. The scarecrow was dressed in…
   a) ☐ a skirt, trousers and gloves.
   b) ☐ shoes, trousers and a hat.
   c) ☐ trousers, gloves and socks.

3. The boys…
   a) ☐ lit the bonfire.
   b) ☐ went down to the village green.
   c) ☐ were scared.

4. Guy Fawkes…
   a) ☐ began to cry.
   b) ☐ tried to kill the king.
   c) ☐ comforted the girl.

Episode 2

Put the sentences into the right order.

1. in the loved to of preachers the streets listening York Guy.

Guy loved listening to the preachers in the streets of York.

2. died was had he Guy's eight when father.

Guys father had died when he was eight.

3. a of Stonegate down a in door soldiers house broke Street.

Soldiers broke down a door of a house in S.S.

4. cross a neck priest the wore his around.

The priest wore a cross around his neck.

5. the into hands stocks were and locked priest's wooden feet.

The priest hands and feet were locked into wooden stocks.

Episode 3

There is a mistake in each of the following sentences. Find the wrong keywords and write down the correct words.

1. Some soldiers were carrying small barrels of beer. _gunpowder_

2. Guy used an Ethernet cable to connect the barrels. _rope_ _rope_

3. Very quietly the men painted the city walls. _backed away from_

4. The soldiers took out their cups and ran towards the city. _weapons_

5. After the fall of Calais Guy met the Spanish king, Don Luis. _commander_

6. Guy became an English prince in the Spanish army. _captain_

Episode 4   Crossword

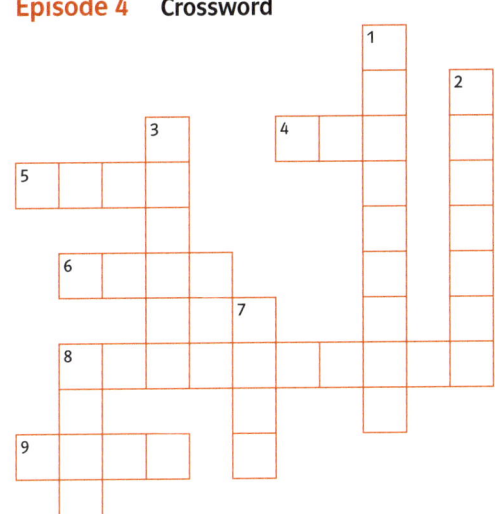

across:

4. a place where you get drinks and food
5. a string to light explosives
6. to end somebody's life by force
8. the State Opening of …
9. to swear an … of secrecy

down:

1. a very explosive substance
2. a person who works for somebody, e.g. does the cooking or cleaning
3. room underneath a house
7. ruler of a country
8. another word for *strategy*

Episode 5

Read episodes 3 – 5 again and have a look at the following speech bubbles. Who says these things? Write down the names of the characters.

> My name is John Johnson, my lord.

1. _G.F_

> We will kill the King of England.

> I am fighting for the Pope.

2. _S.F_

3. _R.C._

> From now on, we will call you Guido.

4. _T.P._

> I have rented a storage room in the cellars under the House of Lords.

5. _____

Episode 6

Read Episode 6 and answer the following questions.

a) How many men are there in the back room of the *Duck and Drake*?

_13_

b) What do all the men have in common (two things)?

They want to kill the King and catholics

c) When does the State Opening of Parliament take place?

_____

d) What does Keyes suggest?

_____

e) Who does Catesby grab by the collar of his coat and why?

_____

Episode 7

Read the summary and fill in the missing words.

warn – Opening of Parliament – betray – brother-in-law – blow up – Catholic –
inform – return – plot – burn – messenger

Lord Monteagle is Tresham's _brother-in-law_ and a _Catholic_ .
He is currently in his house in Huston but he has to _return_ to London
soon for the _opening_ . Suddenly a _messenger_ arrives with a letter.
A *friend* _warned_ him not to attend Parliament. Something will happen
at the State Opening and Monteagle thinks that there is a _plot_ to kill
the king. He believes that there is a plan to _blow up_ Parliament. However,
he does not _burn_ the letter as the secret sender wanted him to do. Out
of fear and for his own good fortune he _informed_ the conspirators. Lord
Monteagle decides to _inform_ King James. _betrays_

Episode 8

Unscramble the following words from episode 8 and translate them into German.

1. slcipti — _politics_
2. visdora — _advisor_ — _Berater_
3. cocesnusiso — _succesion_ — _Erfolg_
4. oltp — _plot_ — _Verschwörung_
5. epsis — _spies_ — _Spione_
6. rroaitt — _traitor_
7. fcsnenoosi — _____
8. aftih — _faith_ — _Glaube_

Episode 9

What happens first? Put these sentences into the correct order.

a) ☐ The soldiers found a fuse and matches in Guy's pockets.

b) ☐ A soldier found the gunpowder behind a pile of coal.

c) ☐ Fawkes gave the captain his sword.

d) ☐ Guy had been stopped by soldiers but they had let him go.

e) ☐ Fawkes carried the last barrel of gunpowder into the cellar.

f) ☐ The captain arrested Guy Fawkes.

g) ☐ A soldier asked Guy what he was doing.

Episode 10

True or false? Circle the answer.

a) Guy Fawkes gives the Lord Chief Justice his real name.   T / F

b) Fawkes has a bleeding nose and he is hungry.   T / F

c) He looks out of the window and sees the Tower of London outside.   T / F

d) He says that he is the servant of Thomas Percy.   T / F

e) The Lord Chief Justice does not believe him.   T / F

f) Guy admitted that he wanted to kill King James.   T / F

g) The Lord Chief Justice thinks that Guy is a soldier.   T / F

h) There were forty-six barrels of gunpowder in the cellar.   T / F

i) Torture is not allowed in England.   T / F

j) The king orders the Chief Justice to torture Guy Fawkes.   T / F

Episode 11

Match the sentence halves.

1. Guido signed his name	a) and fell unconscious.
2. Guy had suffered so much pain	b) pushed him towards the gallows.
3. Soldiers carried him into the yard	c) standing on a wooden stage.
4. Guido closed his eyes	d) at the bottom of the confession.
5. A man poured a bucket	e) his neck snap and break.
6. Guy Fawkes plotted to blow up the	f) that he felt like he was dead.
7. Guy Fawkes was	g) of cold water over his head.
8. The executioner	h) King of England. A traitor.
9. The crowd gasped. He felt	i) and tied him to a wooden panel.

Episode 12

Who is who?

1. Guido Fawkes	a) rented the storage room under the House of Lords
2. Thomas Percy	b) Guy's father (stepfather)
3. Robert Catesby	c) Secretary of State
4. John Johnson	d) Tresham's brother-in-law
5. Denis Bainbridge	i) King of England
6. Lord Monteagle	f) Spanish commander
7. The Earl of Northumberland	g) captain in the Spanish army
8. Robert Cecil	h) a conspirator who owns a house in Lambeth
9. The Archbishop of Canterbury	i) Percy's patron
10. Don Luis de Velasco	j) King of Spain
11. James	k) Guy's false name as servant of Thomas Percy
12. Philip	l) leader of the Church of England

The characters

gunpowder Schießpulver
plot Verschwörung
annual ['ænjuəl] jährlich
effigy ['efɪdʒi] Bildnis
involved mit etw. zu tun haben
to blow up sth etw. sprengen
conspiracy [kən'spɪrəsi] Komplott
to replace ersetzen
blame [bleɪm] Schuld
to expose enthüllen, aufdecken
peer Angehöriger des Hochadels
to receive [rɪ'siːv] erhalten
to execute hinrichten
chief advisor Hauptberater
Secretary of State Minister
to remain in power im Amt bleiben
surrounded by umgeben von
to store lagern
goods Waren
conspirator Verschwörer

Episode 1

scarecrow Vogelscheuche
apart from abgesehen von
good shape guter Verfassung
to wipe [waɪp] abwischen
item Gegenstand
amazing unglaublich, toll
bonfire Freudenfeuer
glove Handschuh
doll Puppe
branch Zweig, Ast
to light (lit, lit) anzünden
to gather sich versammeln
to blaze [bleɪz] lodern

Guy eine Guy Fawkes Puppe
punishment Bestrafung
to carry on weiterhin tun
to deserve verdienen

Episode 2

preacher Prediger
salvation Erlösung
glory *hier:* Himmelreich
chores Hausarbeiten
to charge stürmen
to drag zerren, schleifen
beyond jenseits
to lock sperren, abschließen
stocks Pranger
to mutter [mʌtə] murmeln
prayer Gebet

Episode 3

cover Schutz
to creep (crept, crept) kriechen
barrel Fass
to guard [gɑːd] bewachen
below unterhalb
fuse [fjuːz] Zündschnur
to retreat sich zurückziehen
dawn Morgendämmerung
town hall Rathaus
to praise loben
similar ähnlich

Episode 4

to rest ruhen
hilt Griff
sword [sɔːd] Schwert
robber Räuber

innkeeper Gastwirt
to approach auf jdn zukommen
to lead führen
to embrace [ɪmˈbreɪs] umarmen
to rent mieten
to supply [səˈplaɪ] versorgen
to interrupt unterbrechen
to dig graben
to swear schwören
oath Schwur, Eid

Episode 5

progress Fortschritt
patron Schirmherr, Wohltäter
suspicious [səˈspɪʃəs] misstrauisch
satisfied zufrieden
storage room Stauraum

Episode 6

huddled zusammengedrängt
to postpone verschieben, aufschieben
to recognise erkennen
pale blass, bleich
courage [ˈkʌrɪdʒ] Mut
innocent unschuldig
to betray verraten
to wound [wuːnd] verwunden
to grab schnappen, greifen
collar Kragen

Episode 7

to head back zurückgehen
sealed verschlossen, versiegelt
to bear [beə] hegen, tragen
to devise erfinden, ausdenken
present [ˈprezənt] anwesend

blow Schlag
to burst into hereinstürzen
chamber [tʃeɪmbə] Kammer
matter Angelegenheit
all along die ganze Zeit
opportunity Gelegenheit
quizzically fragend
influence Einfluss
court [kɔːt] Hof
to sparkle funkeln
delight Freude

Episode 8

to be an old hand ein alter Hase
succession to the throne Thronfolge
to arrest verhaften
evidence Beweis(material)
traitor Verräter
confession Geständnis
to renounce abschwören
faith Glaube

Episode 9

log Holzscheit
to raise [reɪz] (hoch)heben
to hesitate [ˈhezɪteɪt] zögern
to beat besiegen
to draw (drew, drawn) ziehen
to hand sth to sb jdm etw. übergeben
to reveal [rɪˈviːl] aufdecken
to knock over umstoßen
stack Stapel
cord Schnur
match Streichholz

Glossary

Episode 10

Lord Chief Justice Lordoberrichter
scar Narbe
windowsill Fenstersims
statement Aussage
to handle umgehen mit
entire gesamt, ganz
to persuade [pə'sweɪd] überreden
torture Folter
necessary nötig
order Befehl
rack Folterbank
to bow sich verneigen

Episode 11

quill Schreibfeder
to suffer ['sʌfə] (er)leiden
wooden panel Holzpaneel
to attach befestigen, anhängen
to whip die Peitsche geben
unconscious ohnmächtig
bucket [bʌkɪt] Eimer, Kübel
to succeed erfolgreich sein
gallows Galgen
noose [nuːs] Schlinge
to settle *hier:* sich legen
to face *hier:* ertragen
effort Anstrengung
desperate verzweifelt
to snap brechen, knacken

Episode 12

beloved heißgeliebt
stall Stand, Bude
square [skweə] Platz
to attempt versuchen

assassination Attentat, Ermordung
intervention Eingreifen
magnificent hervorragend
nursery rhyme Kinderlied
treason Verrat
before long binnen Kurzem

Additional information

effectively im Grunde
oppression Unterdrückung
to be considered *hier:* angesehen werden als
devout [dɪ'vaʊt] fromm
to excommunicate aus der Kirchengemeinschaft ausschließen
to request um etwas bitten
heir [eər] Erbe
divide Kluft
to remain bleiben
to achieve erreichen
to establish gründen, etablieren
allegiance [ə'liːdʒənts] Loyalität
in particular insbesondere
influential einflussreich

to revert [rɪ'vɜːt] zurückkehren
several mehrere
to adopt annehmen
capture ['kæptʃə] Gefangennahme
put on trial vor Gericht gebracht
doubt [daʊt] Zweifel
guilty schuldig
high treason Hochverrat
sentenced verurteilt
to behead köpfen
to chop zerhacken
stake Scheiterhaufen
to spare verschonen